The Water Gospel

The Water Gospel
A Long Poem

Tom Gibbs

Introduction by Larry E. Maze

TEKTŌN PRESS

Published by TEKTŌN Press
P. O. Box 93
St. Mary of the Woods, IN 47876

For my mother,
Anagene Wooten Gibbs

and

For my mother-in-law,
Mabel Lyons Thompson

Water is the only substance that exists in all three of the physical states of matter—liquid, gas, and solid—and can change from state to state at various stages of the water cycle in the blink of an eye and over millions of years; and because the water cycle is truly a cycle, there is no beginning or end.
–Basic science

We forget the water cycle and the life cycle are one.
–Jacques Cousteau

The highest goodness is like water.
Water graces all without discord.
It flows to places others reject.
It nears the Tao.   –Lao Tzu

We may not be God, but we are of God, even as a little drop of water is of the ocean.   –Gandhi

and he shall come unto us as the rain, as the latter and the former rain unto the earth.   –Hosea 6: 3

Therefore with joy shall you draw water out of the wells of salvation.   –Isaiah 12: 3

Introduction

"Gospel" comes from the Greek language and means "good news." I think it loses something in the translation. Because for us good news ranges from not having it rain when our umbrella is somewhere else to having a clear biopsy. It might be that company is coming—or that company isn't coming. But "good news" hardly conveys an experience of transformative dimensions.

It's helpful to remember that *Matthew, Mark, Luke,* and *John* in the Bible were first written for people who knew what deep longing felt like. At least among the Jewish readers of "the Good News" there had been generation after generation of waiting and expecting the fulfillment of prophecy. The life and work of Jesus was *remarkably* good news to those whose lives seemed on hold until the Son of David would appear. For those who wandered the countryside with this itinerate preacher and heard what he said and watched what he did to bring life to those he encountered, this was *incredibly* good news.

But that news could not and cannot be captured by the words used to tell the story of God's own Wisdom residing in this man from Nazareth. For the people of his own day, it seemed that to be in the presence of Jesus was to be in the presence of God. It had to do with what he said and did, but more so, it had to do with what he awakened in the Soul of everyone he met who didn't flee in terror of having their own Soul awakened. There were words spoken, some of which have been captured by the gospel writers of the first century. But there was more. This man could stir one to the very depth of humanity where words always fail to convey the experience.

In our time and in our part of the world words are not supposed to fail. What separates us from simpler species with whom we share this planet is language. We use the gift of language to analyze mystery and ambiguity which we falsely believe we can ultimately overcome. We want our language to be clear and specific and carry the power of "knowing." We forget that language is symbolic; that it points beyond itself to a reality that is almost always much larger than words can convey. We speak words of love to those precious few who bring meaning and depth to our lives, yet the words are never quite adequate. We use words to codify how our civilization is supposed to function, yet one glance at a law library tells us that it is never quite as clear as we wanted it to be. We write scientific reports knowing that the tiniest variation will change the results of our careful testing…and there are countless variations.

Like all things, our blessing of language carries its own curse. The light that shines when words come out clear and helpful, casts its own shadow if only to remind us that words are symbols always pointing to that which is beyond.

Over time, a way of reading holy and sanctified words has emerged that fails to remember this reality of symbol. It seems strange that in the religious realm where symbol is so important, many still seek absolute applications of what they read in holy books. Some reduce religion to bumper sticker language: God Said It; I Believe It; That's It!

Holy writing above all writing should remind us that the words were written with fear and trembling so readers in all ages would find the words transparent so that Wisdom and Truth, never captured by our words, might be received. Jesus *always* used language about the Eternal Kingdom he saw dawning that was symbolic—language clever enough to keep his hearers from jumping to conclusions. It was always, "The Kingdom of God is *like*…" It's like this or it's like that. It's like when things get turned upside down and the weak are revealed as the strong; the poor as rich; the simple as wise; and little children as the example for faith. It's like tax collectors becoming key disciples and despised Samaritans showing forth the Kingdom before the rest of us. But never does Jesus say, "The Kingdom of God *is*…." The Kingdom of God extends beyond our best language.

Tom Gibbs clearly knows all this about us and our words. As I read and reread *The Water Gospel* I am drawn to that place that simply refuses to allow this to be another report on Jesus. It is the language of metaphor -- metaphor as deep as the water into which the poet invites us. For us water is life at any level we might choose to think. From womb to grave we live because water sustains us. Because there is water, this green and blue planet is alive with more life than we can think about. Is it any wonder that the Soul has found water to be its favorite metaphor!

The Jesus you will meet in this elegant poem is the same one you have met when reading the gospels of Holy Scripture. You will recognize that story contained in this story. But you will be invited away from the temptation of reading as though there are certain facts to be known about this man! You will be invited into the place where poets live, where words invite us to swim in deep Wisdom. You will travel with the Psalmist who sings "Deep calls out to deep at the thunder of your cataracts; all your waves and your billows have gone over me."[1]

The Psalmist would have found it absurd to be asked to explain what happens when deep calls out to deep. How could he possibly know what that could mean for anyone other than himself? Indeed, he could hardly explain the experience for himself, which is why he uses the language of the poet! Yet, some have surrendered the Truth that rises from our own Divine center to those who tell them what the truth really is. Life somehow

---

[1] Psalm 42:7

seems clearer, maybe even safer, when we project our own deep inner journey onto religious figures who tell us what the Kingdom of God supposedly is and what we must do about it.

This was the world of the first century as well. Holy living had been projected onto the priesthood, the Sadducees, and the Pharisees. And into such a world came Jesus who invited his followers to go in where they would find the Divine center where deep meets deep. Faced with absolutes, either this or that, he was likely to tell a parable where things were not quite so clear. Faced with regulations, he asked questions about the spirit behind the regulation. Faced with the agonizing belief that God was wholly other and our fate was to be forever separate from the ground of our being, Jesus spoke of the branches of the vine taking life from what the vinegrower has planted. "I am the true vine, and my father is the vinegrower … you are the branches."[2] Life connected to the Lifegiver is life immersed in Living Water.

The Jesus you will meet in these pages is one who knew that Living Water is not owned by him or any holy system or any religion. The living water rises up from within the Soul of every part of Creation and draws us to deep truths about who we are and how we are called to join the dance of Creation.

_____

[2] John 15:1-5

Not that the living water
is outside them
and inside them, not that the
the kingdom they seek
is no kingdom
but a whole new realm of
possibility, no more mine
than theirs. Still,
every place we go,
I bring the word, simple
and clear as water.

If they open their ears
to hear;
the same way they part their lips
to drink,
they'll know the word
as sure as their tongues
taste the end of thirst.

They'll know that what they want
from me and can have,
they can want from themselves
and can have, too.

This is Jesus who lived in Living Water but
knew that it was intended for all humanity. This
is the man from Nazareth whose longing sounds
like yours and mine. But more than that, this is
Jesus who awakens the deep Wisdom that abides
not in some, but in all. "Wisdom is created with

the faithful in the womb. She made among human beings an eternal foundation, and among their descendants she will abide faithfully."[3]

> They could know
> that the wonders they seek
> they carry already
> in their hearts, that the
> water of life is the water
> of life and their own breath
> is the spirit
> that moves across its face.

I'm forever grateful to poets. They share with composers, artists, dancers and others the language of metaphor and symbol. The Wisdom to which they lead us is like water, always flowing to the deepest places.

Larry E. Maze

---

[3] Ecclesiasticus 1:14-15

The Water Gospel

I: A cup of rain

The first of these latter rains,
a chorus of whispers,
wakes me,
calls me to the door.

Something of me
goes out. Something of me
enters.

In that strange passage,
that quiet exchange, a reverie
deep as prayer.   10

Night comes fragrant,
water and dust.
The long dry wait
passes, the new season rises.

Almond and lilies,
vine, and the grasses in the field
drink this new water,
wait for the light
and by the grace of the two
bring back   20
leaf and flower.

At middle watch, the watchmen
talk in shouts and laughter
that sail on the breeze
through the rain,
their words muted, their tone
clear, joyful.

Behind me, the room
flares with sudden light
and as quick   30
dims to a soft glow.

I think she's risen
to stir the coals in the brazier,
hammered from a lost shield,
but she still sleeps.

Another stirs
the embers to flame,
wears a simlah that glows
marble-white
in this new light   40
like the radiance
the moon
borrows from the sun.

The messenger comes
in the music of wind and rain,
no need to tell me
not to fear. The one
long expected to return
announces my next passage,
calls me to my own
new season, to this
other holy thing being born
as this water
breaks over the earth from
out of heaven.

The same voice
my mother first heard
at the well
says the thirst I've known
since boyhood
can end.

The water jar is full, but the
cups are empty.

Work done with my hands
brought out grace and function
from wood.

The new work is the word
and the living water
carries it like a stream
to shape the heart's purpose
with grace.

I accept the work
and receive the word
as easy as a cup of rain.

II: A new skin

I come down from Galilee
to find my wilderness cousin,
the baptist,
waist deep in the Jordan,
wrapped and girded
in skins and hides,   80
waiting to see the
pronouncements of angels
fulfilled.

What I've heard
is true.

The wind
moves on the water,
comes again to rewrite
the beginning.

His voice cries out   90
on that same breath rising,
telling of the ghost.

I try to see him, but he's
lost in sunlight and
all I see is light,
a skin of fire on the surface of
the water, a glaze
like goat's butter on new loaves.

The water
becomes light.   100

Near the river's edge, I walk
among the others,
brush past them
as if they weren't there,
the way a child might run to a father's call
when evening draws near and the
world falls away with each sure step
until the house
is safely reached.

I step into the water,   110
cool on my feet
and other waters return to me
as alive as this.

The recent rains
that filled this river
still sing to me my waking
to this new water,
but I recall
other waters
and now I know   120
they were just as sacred.

Each sweet drink
from the well in Nazareth,
cool on my lips
after play or work.

Gentle summer waves
in Gennesaret
smooth on my skin
when I swam near Magdala.

Wash water   130
silk in my hands
when I put down my tools.

All these common waters
taken for granted
feel as alive as this river,
as if water
were always a new skin.

Each step I take
takes me deeper,
nearer the dark origins,
backwards,
that I can now come forward,
deeper, that I can rise up
to become who I am.

Each step closer
until in my turn I'm immersed
and when I'm borne up
out of the water,
the light is all over me,
a new skin,
and the taste of it,
wet and cool on my lips,
ends my thirst,
becomes my word.

III: How this begins

After forty days
in the wilderness,
the desert far south of here,
with only water and the ghost
to sustain me,

rocks begin to resemble loaves   160
and I wonder…

But before I try my hand
at what I know is at hand,
I accept that the mystery
is no conjuror's trick
and neither in me nor of me,
to serve myself alone.

And though it would be so easy
to make these stones
be bread, I turn back evil   170
with the word
and leave the stones
to the earth.

Twice more I'm taunted
but I won't test
my faith in angels
or embrace kingdoms
that time and men can ruin.

Here in Cana, my own mother
asks for wine.   180

Is this some other trap
or test, or only
a sad vanity,
some thoughtless pride
to make a show of who I am
or who she is?

After Jordan and the desert,
how can she ask this of me?

Who am I to her
or she to me   190
now that I go
to my own time
which is still to come?

She tells the stewards to do
what I say
and leaves the rest to me.

I can't refuse such faith.

I tell the stewards to fill the
waterpots with water
and I wonder,   200

Who could ask
for more than this?

but I say, Draw it back out.
and they draw out wine.

This is how this begins,
with water,
like everything else.

Wine will satisfy
this revelry
but only living water   210
can quench true thirst.

When my own hour comes,
what will they
give me to drink?

IV: This water and that water

This hour erases shadows,
light is heat, heat
is a shimmer, a veil
between this well stone
and the bluffs of Gerizim.

Her singing precedes her as   220
her stride
plays her earrings and neck chains,
bracelets and anklets
like pipe notes
on the rhythm of her sway.

She sends down her jar
at her task as if I'm no more
than a tree or a stone,
except for a glance,
curious and wary,   230
as she draws up the water.

She startles and draws back
when I speak to her,
propriety being what it is.

A simple request for water,
a small drink,
falls like a sword between us
and she asks how I can so casually
break tradition
that forbids cordial commerce   240
between our two peoples.

I make of my hand a cup,
dip water from her jar
and drink.

Draw up water
from any well in Jerusalem,
as she draws water
from this well.

Both waters come
from heaven and earth,   250
both waters
sustain us all,
man or woman, prophet or
profligate, Jew or Samaritan.

Whatever she's done,
however this life has
made her way for her,
she offers no guile
but lets truth
carry her words, as love   260
carries forgiveness.

She says my words are like
the puzzles of prophets.

My words are another water,
living water,
everlasting water
that bears us all
into life. She asks
for this water.

A cup is a cup, a well   270
is a well. My words
are her words, this water is her
water. The well of salvation
is in us all
for us to draw this water from,
just as we draw that water
from the earth.

This is the spirit
and truth: This water and that water
are one. Water is water.   280

On open mountain or
in temple chambers,
water is water
and the spirit moves there. Factions
only muddy the water,
darken the spirit.

V: One thing for the other

Go back to the beginning
when the spirit moves
on the face of the waters.

It's that simple.   290
It all begins there.

Day and night
divided over them. Heaven raised
and cradled
between the waters, under
and above. Seas
gathered under heaven
and from them
this land, this earth, and here
as in heaven   300
water has no end.

Rain falls, renews
and greens the land,
runs full the rivers and the
streams, fills
the spring,
the well, and the cistern,
gives up its ghost
but comes again.

On the tops of mountains,   310
water is solid
as any stone, as
any one of us.

Go back to the beginning,
back to the face of the waters
where spirit moves.

Water, cloud, and ice,
one as easy as the other, wine
as easy as water,
as easy for you as for me.   320

The difference
is in the hesitation,
the shadow of doubt,
the fear to let go
of one thing for the other.

Take the boat out again
into deep water,
cast and drag the nets
once more. The fisherman
hesitates   330
in that shadow and complains
before he shrugs and takes
my word for it,
unable to take his own.

The nets come up full
to breaking.

It's as simple as that.
Faith in the knowledge
and knowing faith.
As easy for him

as for me, as for anyone.
Why else am I here?

340

VI: Even after the water calms

Near the lake they press me,
want more from me
than they're willing to want or ask
from themselves, all of them.

The ones who follow
and the ones who crowd around
waiting to see
some clear evidence that I am   350
who they say I am. That I am
who I am.

They wait for stones to become
loaves, their water
to become wine,
their ills of this world to be
cleansed
as surely as wind erases
what's written in dust.

They wait for the great spectacles   360
they hear about
and those are the words that go round
in whispers.

Not that the living water
is outside them
and inside them, not that the
kingdom they seek
is no kingdom
but a whole new realm of
possibility, no more mine   370
than theirs. Still,
every place we go,
I bring the word, simple
and clear as water.

If they open their ears
to hear,
the same way they part their lips
to drink,
they'll know the word
as sure as their tongues   380
taste the end of thirst.

They'll know that what they want
from me and can have,
they can want from themselves
and can have, too.

But they never hear.
They always thirst.
They trade faith for their eyes
as if seeing
is the only believing.   390

We leave and set sail
for the other side, the ship
a cradle in the arms of
the waves.

Before it rocks me into
a deeper sleep, they wake me
from a dream of clear pools
and sparrows.

They tremble, cry
like children, wail   400
that the wind has raised
the water into storm,
that we'll all soon drown.

Again
I'm stunned.

Even the ones who listen
won't hear.
Even after the water calms,
they wonder about me
instead of themselves, about
the spectacle
instead of the faith.

410

VII: Still, they seek for wonders

Long-sought solitude, twilight
above the lake. The searchers for wonders
sent off to their homes,
the apostles
sent on across the water.

The breeze, sweet with the fragrance
of earth cooling and
night coming, restores   420
this delicate balance that holds me
both a part and apart.

Here is silence and silence
is my prayer, the stream
into and out of my heart that
carries me in living water
from where I came, to where
I am, to where I go,
toward grace, by will, into
pure faith.   430

Let silence become the word for
what has no word. Let water
be its form and voice
here in this life
a mystery we all
recognize and use
daily. Water to bathe,
water to drink.

Each common act
a prayer in itself   440
that makes of the outer and the inner
a perfect harmony, pure peace,
and faith. If they knew
water and silence,
they could know themselves
as clearly as I do.

They could know
that the wonders they seek
they carry already
in their hearts, that the   450
water of life is the water
of life and their own breath
is the spirit
that moves across its face.

It's there they'll find
the wonder they seek,
and the heart's silence.

The last of the sun's oil flares,
burns out,
brings down the heavens 460
to full dark
under a breath-taking shimmer of stars,

and they seek for wonders.

The air cools, the breeze rises.
A deeper breath
crosses the surface of the lake.
Dark clouds
tumble against the night, invisible,
except as stars vanish
in broken lines along ragged edges. 470

Storm blows up the air, excites
the water, drives up a wind
out of the breeze. Lightning
burns open the night
in blue fragments,

and they seek for wonders.

They cry out,
children whose fear
devours what little faith
they have and still
they don't understand.

I go down to the water
and walk to them.

They moan louder,
as if I'm already the ghost, as if
what they see
defies their faith and this
is the greater burden, that the ones
who believe
have no faith. When they listen,
they don't hear. When they look,
they never see.

This water is your water
as much as mine. Come to me
and see.

480

490

The water in you
and around you
is the same water from the beginning
to the end. The fisherman
tries the leap,   ₅₀₀
but can't complete it
and sinks.

When you see in the eyes
and the falling face
faith dissipate,
gone in the wind,
you see the spirit lost
as doubt enters,
heavy as rock. You see
the tenuous thread between us   ₅₁₀
and our maker
break, and you wonder,
as in marvel, at the dark distance
from the maker such a fall
takes us.

They crowd around
ready to believe again.
What I've done
amazes them. What they didn't do
is already forgotten.   ₅₂₀

The storm passes
beyond the lake, leaves in its wake
the stars unaltered,
the waters calm, the wind
a pleasant breeze. Still,
they seek for wonders
greater than these.

VIII: Living rivers

The days are lost
when I could work alone
to a timeless music of birdsongs, shouts 530
and laughter in the streets,
and the steady close rhythm of my
drawknife
bringing the finished lintel out of
the rough timber.

Now my work is less with my hands
than my heart,
and as sure as my tools were, in my
hands,
my words must find a rhythm 540
as clear and certain as the stream
from the spring
that replenishes each of us.

But my words meet resistance
the way the blade
halts hard against the knot
or the stream goes sluggish
in the stagnant pool.

The ones who gather
raise their voices in a foul and   550
dissonant sound that confounds
the simple truth. They argue
about who I am or
who I'm not. They listen
but never hear, talk
their mouths dry
and leave a thirst
they could quench themselves if
they only would.

If they heard, they'd hear   560
the silence
and the word,
clear as spring water.

They'd hear my words
and in their own heart's silence
know them as their own, know
that they too are of the same
spring,
are the same spring,
that feeds the rivers   570
of the living waters.

Water gives its ghost to heaven,
returns as rain. The word
gives its spirit
and comes back. Water
is my metaphor.

IX: Both food and water

For a moment,
quiet holds only soft sounds
in its net. The river
runs slow in its banks. Grasses   580
translate the breeze
into whispers.

The low voices
of three men in a boat
drift south. The men wave
but nothing more.

I strike a pomegranate
against a stone to pierce
its skin. Food and water both
tumble into my hands   590
as brilliant as rubies
but worth so much more. An oasis
in a single sphere.

Others gather near me
as if the wind
has called them here
and maybe it has. Some say
they know me.
Some say they've seen me
work signs. Some scoff   600
and want proof. They all
want to see.

Confine faith to only
what you see
and you'll never
be certain of faith.

Can you see the orchard
in my hand?

Weigh only one of these seeds
and record its weight   610
as this or that
according to the scale
and you'll leave its weight
unweighed.

A dry seed in dry ground
is a body without soul.
All that comes from it
is dust.

Sow these seeds on the ground. If only one
germinates,   620
it doubles its weight. Plant it in soil
fertile with possibility,
make your hand a cup
and scatter this river like rain
over the new growth.

Day by day
its weight increases
until the root
becomes the shoot, the shoot
the sapling and from the sapling   630
the tree grows
into its own. The tree flowers,
bears fruit
and that fruit is both food
and water.

You know this.
It's a sign you see
with your own eyes
season after season.

You know the great waters
grow the seed of the land
into the fruitful fields.

What does the seed weigh now?

X: Alive as the watered earth

Rancor. Voices rise inside
the temple, hands
take up stones. I say only the truth,
my words clear as well water.
The ones who waver in doubt
make lies of the words,
poison of the water.   650

To offer the cup is one thing,
to accept the cup
is quite another.

Under the din of this disbelief,
I escape unseen.

In the fresh, clear air,
warble and chirp
tie together
the thrums and rhythms of this
plain song life,   660
the laughs and shouts of children
run through the streets
a stream of joyful noise.

Sorrow finds its psalm in the
beggar's cant. His cry rises
that mercy might work
from the heart and faith
come from the spirit. In balance,
the two find a harmony
that heals in whole notes,   670
clear as water drops
on fountain stones.

In the tradition of the first
rain bound with the dust
of the ground, mercy
binds my spit with dirt
to make a man whole.
Blind from the womb,
he receives this clay on faith,
and the word.   680

Sent to the pool of Siloam,
he doesn't hesitate,
but goes with assurance to
wash the mud away
and rises from the water
bathed in light
and seeing, filled
with the breath of new life,
his spirit alive
as the watered earth, his eyes   690
open like blossoms
to a new world, a new vision,
with no dark sorrow
any more at all.

XI: Body and soul

No one enters
except through water.
We all follow water out of the dark,
out of the teardrop womb.
We follow the surge and spring forth
bathed in light, wet on our skin.   700

King or beggar,
we follow the water out.

Water is the savior
in this dry land, the blood
and the spirit. Without it
is without life,
true since the beginning.

This is my parable,
my metaphor, the oasis
in the desert.   710

Earth gives up its breath
to the heavens. Rain falls
and olive, almond, and vine renew
and ripen.

Streams fill and flow into rivers,
rivers to the lakes and to
the seas. All of this eternal
since creation.

In winter's breath,
water is ice, rare crystals   720
fragile as the flight of birds,
solid as bone,
for a time.

Spring brings it back to the
waters of the earth
and to the breath of heaven.

This rhythm, this motion,
quenches rich and poor alike,
cleanses Greek and Roman,
Samaritan and Jew alike.   730

It's a common task
to wash their feet
and offer in place of parable
a simple act of love
even though they won't understand
or even know how it is
that who they think I am
could stoop so low
as to serve them.

Why should now   740
be any different?
It all takes time,
but this time
is short for me now.

By this common kindness,
they might come to know
that master is servant and servant
master,
that by washing their feet,
the savior is saved.   750

A simple prayer.

What I have, they have. What I give,
they should give too
and be as selfless in their giving.
What I am, they are too.

This water washes body and soul
and each breath
catches the spirit,
raises it to heaven
holy and everlasting.   760

XII: By the rivers of water

A breeze in the cedars
the sound of early rain
or murmurs
on the breath of angels.

Linnets and finches
twitter in the cover of mustard,
tithe mint fresh in the air.
The temple light waits in the olive
to be pressed into service.

In this new watered garden,   770
I meet my sorrow with tears
and prayer.

Tears are only one of the heart's
weathers. They fall
one at a time
rare as a star
that falls across heaven
or they rain down hard
out of this storm
where the life I've had   780
crashes against the life I give
for the life I'm given.

Tears taste like the sea,
a reminder that even
our changing moods are water
and as ancient
as creation itself.

Prayer is the weather
to calm the storm,
settle the rough seas,   790
bring the heart to silence
and silence to the heart.
Then we can hear
the one voice among the many.

As in the beginning,
wind moves on the waters,
carries their breath up
into the sun's light until its heat
draws that breath to heaven
where clouds gather like   800
holy ghosts and are
blessed back to earth
in the body of new water.

This is the source
of rivers and streams,
life-giving waters,
the precious cycle of life itself.
The blessing of rain.

Seeds send down their roots
and the roots their shoots   810
up from the dark, fertile earth.
The blessing of rain.

Buds unfold and blossoms open.
The blessing of rain.

This is my own cup
come again, come at last.
This is my own hour
nearing. This season
is my own harvest,
my winter   820
and my spring.

I return to from where I came.
Simple truth as common as
water and as precious.
It is what it is. I am
what I am. I finish
what is begun
so that in the end
is the beginning.

Let the others sleep, their 830
bodies and the weight
of this hour
too heavy
for their souls to carry,
and the others,
let them fill their plots.

I'd have this cup
pass from me,
but what I'd gain
falls far short 840
of what I'd forfeit.

In this garden
my ghost
becomes holy,
the watered garden
waiting to bloom,
the spring
that never runs dry, the tree
by the rivers of water.

I bear the fruit 850
of my own season,
food
and the living water,
seeds
for the new garden.